Luther advised . . .

"After you have taught them  up the Large Catechism an .... also a richer and fuller knowledge."

Martin Luther, Preface to his Small Catechism (1529)

. . . and he was right.

Here is what laypeople experience with *Studying Luther's Large Catechism: A Workbook for Christian Discipleship*:

"The Large Catechism study guide made it so I will never say the Lord's Prayer again the same. Now I say it with more meaning. This is a good guide for all believers to review their faith in God."

L.M.O.

"At confirmation age, Luther's Small Catechism is the perfect fit for instruction in the fundamentals of the Christian faith. But few adult Lutherans have taken the time to study the Large Catechism in depth by thinking through the biblical support for Lutheran Christian doctrine. We enjoyed going back to catechism class led by Dr. Ryan MacPherson using his study guide to Luther's Large Catechism. The study is challenging and edifying to anyone who loves being a lifelong learner. An added bonus is the mutual encouragement and stimulating discussions that flow from the study."

Herman and Cheryl Harstad

"*Studying Luther's Large Catechism* helped to enrich our faith. The pointed questions for each lesson led us back to the appropriate sections of the Large Catechism and to the verses of the Holy Bible which support them. The opportunity to study the Large Catechism, and through it the Holy Bible, with a group of fellow Christians also was a blessed opportunity to deepen our relationships with others."

John and Stephanie Merseth

A Lutheran Tradition for Nearly 500 Years

"In the Catechism we have simple affirmations of that which constitutes Christian belief and life, and this is its chief merit, which lifts it above the age which saw its birth and gives it a timeless quality. It is as one has remarked, 'a booklet which a theologian never finishes learning, and a Christian never finishes living.' It is as up to date in 1929 as it was in 1529.

"Luther wrote his Catechism chiefly for the Christian home, in order that the Christian homes should again become home-churches, where the housefathers were both house-priests and house-teachers. It was intended especially for the home, to be a home book to be used by parents for their own profit and as a textbook for the instruction of the young. At the head of each of the five chief parts of the Catechism stand these words: 'As the head of the family should teach it in all simplicity to his household.'"

Joseph B. Unseth, "The Right Use of the Catechism" (1929)

"Luther's Small Catechism empowered the laity, as members of the priesthood of the baptized, to exercise their role in judging doctrine. By being accountable to the Small Catechism, a Lutheran pastor was thereby accountable to his congregation. In the Large Catechism, Martin Luther modeled in greater detail how pastors and laity submit themselves to Holy Scripture, but even as that catechism takes them onto a more advanced level, they forever remain students of the simple truths summarized in the Small Catechism. Dr. MacPherson's *Studying Luther's Large Catechism* once again points the church back to these great treasures by presenting study questions that guide both pastors and laity, in both church and home, through Luther's catechetical method."

Pastor David Jay Webber
Scottsdale, Arizona

Studying Luther's Large Catechism:

A Workbook for Christian Discipleship

Ryan C. MacPherson, Ph.D.

www.hausvater.org

The Hausvater Project

Mankato, Minnesota

www.hausvater.org

Studying Luther's Large Catechism: A Workbook for Christian Discipleship, by Ryan C. MacPherson, Ph.D.

Credits and copyright permissions for hymns are indicated throughout this book. Collects (prayers) are from *Evangelical Lutheran Hymnary* (St. Louis: MorningStar, 1996), ©1996 by the Lutheran Synod Book Company, used by permission. Quotations from the Lutheran Confessions are from *Concordia: The Lutheran Confessions, A Reader's Edition of the Book of Concord.* Edited by Paul Timothy McCain. 2d ed. St. Louis: Concordia Publishing House, 2007. ©2007 by Concordia Publishing House. Used by permission.

Cover art: Seal of Martin Luther, *ca.* 1520s, public domain, newly colorized.

ISBN–10: 0983568111

ISBN–13: 978-0-9835681-1-7

Library of Congress Subject Headings

Lutheran Church—Catechisms and Creeds

Lutheran Church—Education

Lutheran Church—Theology

Luther, Martin, 1483–1546

Contents

The Place of Martin Luther and His Catechisms in Church History

Martin Luther (1483–1546) demonstrated through his life what it means for a person to regard Holy Scripture as the supreme judge of one's doctrine and practice. As the father of the Lutheran Reformation, he steadfastly pointed people to the message that Christ alone (*solus Christus*) is their Savior from sin and damnation, that He has redeemed them by God's grace alone (*sola fide*), that people receive these great benefits not through their own works but rather through faith alone (*sola fide*), and that Scripture alone (*sola Scriptura*) must establish every doctrine of the Christian faith. Finding the contemporary state of Christian education to be dangerously poor, Luther published his Small and Large Catechisms in 1529. In these simple handbooks, written for pastors and parents alike, Luther directed his followers to the core teachings of Holy Scripture. In 1577, his followers referred to these catechisms as "'the laymen's Bible' because everything necessary for a Christian to know for salvation is included in them" (*Concordia*, p. 474; Ep Summary, 5). For nearly five centuries now, Christians have continued to treasure Luther's catechisms for that very reason.

How This Study Is Organized

Each lesson in this study includes reading assignments and study questions for participants to complete prior to meeting as a group. When they meet, they can compare their answers and re-read selected portions of the assignment under the direction of their teacher.

Each lesson begins with a liturgical prayer suitable to the topic of that lesson and concludes with a lyrical selection from one of Martin Luther's hymns on the catechism. (Lesson 1 uses a hymn by B. Pedersen, which serves as a summary of Luther's catechetical hymns.) The final section in each lesson summarizes the main points and suggests applications to the participants' lives.

Participants are encouraged to use the edition of Luther's catechisms printed in *Concordia* (see "Supplementary Resources," below). However, other translations also are suitable. This study guide provides not only page references to *Concordia* but also paragraph references that correspond to the numbering scheme used in most editions of the Large Catechism. For example, "pp. 359–61; LC I, 1–29" means paragraph numbers 1 through 29 of Part I of the Large Catechism, as found on pages 359 through 361 of *Concordia*. Participants using other printings of the Large Catechism will be able to locate the corresponding text as paragraphs 1 through 29 of Part I of the Large Catechism, regardless of differences in page numbering.

Supplemental Resources

Concordia   *Concordia: The Lutheran Confessions, A Reader's Edition of the Book of Concord.* Edited by Paul Timothy McCain. 2d ed. St. Louis: Concordia Publishing House, 2007.

ELH   Evangelical Lutheran Synod. *Evangelical Lutheran Hymnary.* St. Louis: MorningStar Music Publishers, 1996.

Cross-references are provided throughout this study to enable the use of a variety of hymnals other than the recommended ELH:

CW   *Christian Worship: A Lutheran Hymnal* (1993)

LBW   *Lutheran Book of Worship* (1982)

LHy   *The Lutheran Hymnary* (1913)

LSB   *Lutheran Service Book* (2006)

LW   *Lutheran Worship* (1982)

TLH   *The Lutheran Hymnal* (1941)

Suggestions for Teachers

This curriculum originated as a summer Bible study that consisted of two sessions lasting six weeks each. Classes met for ninety minutes, one evening per week. Participants were encouraged to read the assigned portions of the Large Catechism and Scripture in advance in order to prepare responses to the study questions. During class, one or a few sentences were *occasionally* read aloud from the Large Catechism for discussion; the Bible passages cited in the study questions *always* were read aloud before discussion.

The participants' ages ranged from about twenty to eighty years. Some were college graduates, but others were not. All had previously been confirmed in the Lutheran church after studying the Small Catechism, but only a few had read the Large Catechism. The participants universally found the bulk of Luther's text to be instantly comprehensible and obviously relevant to their lives. Most importantly, both Luther's writing and the study questions in this curriculum direct readers back to Holy Scripture where all doctrine is firmly established.

Pastors and teachers can easily adapt this course to other formats, including:

• Four sessions of Sunday morning Bible class (lasting forty-five minutes to an hour) on the Lord's Prayer (spreading Lessons 8 and 9 over four sessions by dividing each lesson in half).

- Two sessions of Sunday morning Bible class (lasting forty-five minutes to an hour) on Holy Baptism (covering half of Lesson 10 in each session).

- A high-school level homeschool curriculum lasting one semester (spending one week on each lesson, with parent and child discussing the study questions together).

Instructors do well to remember:

- Everyone in this study can learn whether completing the study questions in advance or not. Therefore, "homework" should be viewed as an opportunity rather than a burden.

- When study questions invite personal application, individual responses should still share a common foundation in the biblical text, rather than celebrate personal interpretations.

- Luther's Large Catechism is to be honored not because Luther wrote it, but because it faithfully presents the chief doctrines of Holy Scripture.

- The Scriptures teach primarily two doctrines: the Law and the Gospel. The Law reveals our sins and our need for forgiveness. The Gospel reveals Christ's salvation for us through His vicarious life, death, and resurrection. The Law brings comfort only in light of the Gospel: we recognize that Christ has fulfilled the Law on our behalf.

- This study guide intentionally connects the Small Catechism, the Large Catechism, and the prayers and hymns of the church into a cohesive whole. Bible study enriches the divine service, and the divine service enriches Bible study.

- God's Word is powerful and changes hearts. Every Bible passage cited in the study questions should be read aloud before participants share their answers. A Bible study must remain first and foremost a *Bible* study.

Instructors may contact the author with any further questions they have. Contact information is provided at the end of this book.

Lesson 1:
Learning and Teaching God's Word

Pray

Lord God, heavenly Father, we thank You that through Your Son Jesus Christ You have sown Your holy Word among us: We pray that You will prepare our hearts by Your Holy Spirit, that we may diligently and reverently hear Your Word, keep it in good hearts, and bring forth fruit with patience; and that we may not incline to sin, but subdue it by Your power, and in all persecutions comfort ourselves with Your grace and continual help; through Your beloved Son, Jesus Christ, our Lord, who lives and reigns with You and the Holy Spirit, one true God, now and forever. Amen.

Veit Dietrich, Collect for Sexagesima Sunday, in *ELH*, Collect #35, p. 151.

Read

• "Editor's Introduction to the Catechisms" (pp. 309–12)

Discuss

1. "Catechism" comes from a Greek word meaning "to echo" or "to sound back and forth." Why is this an appropriate title for Luther's Small Catechism?

2. Luther was not the first person to write a catechism, but his Small Catechism was quite different from earlier catechisms. What were some of those differences? What do those differences reveal about Luther's goals in preparing the catechism?

3. Luther prepared his Small and Large Catechisms initially as a series of sermons on the chief doctrines of Holy Scripture. Then he compiled them into books, and even made a summary poster to be hung in Christian homes. Explain how Luther's visitation of the congregations in Saxony prompted him to exert so much energy in preparing, publishing, and promoting the catechisms.

Read

- "Preface of Dr. Martin Luther," *Small Catechism* (pp. 313–15; SC Preface, 1–27)

Discuss

4. Whom does Luther blame for the inadequate state of Christian education at the time he wrote the Small Catechism (SC Preface, 1–5)?

5. What solutions does Luther propose for the problem of biblical illiteracy (SC Preface, 6–10)?

6. Luther writes, "But those who are unwilling to learn the catechism should be told that they deny Christ and are not Christians" (p. 314; SC Preface, 11). However, Luther also writes, "We are to force no one to believe or to receive the Sacrament" (p. 315; SC Preface, 21). What is Luther trying to say? Are these two statements consistent?

7. What is the relationship between the Small Catechism and the Large Catechism, according to Luther (p. 314; SC Preface, 17–18)?

8. How do Luther's plans for the catechisms fit with Deuteronomy 6:6–9?

Read

- "Preface" and "Short Preface," *Large Catechism* (pp. 351–58; LC Preface, 1–20; LC Short Preface, 1–28)

Discuss

9. For whom did Luther write the Large Catechism (p. 351; LC Preface, 1)? And for whom else (p. 356; LC Short Preface, 1, 4)?

10. Luther identifies several benefits of "catechism study." What are those benefits? How can we be sure that catechism study will provide us with those benefits (LC Preface, 9–16)?

11. Luther writes, "Whoever knows the Ten Commandments perfectly must know all the Scriptures" (p. 354; LC Preface, 17). Later he writes, "For in these three parts [the Ten Commandments, the Apostles' Creed, and the Lord's Prayer], everything that we have in the Scriptures is included in short, plain, and simple terms" (pp. 357–58; LC Short Preface, 18). Finally, he writes, "When these three parts are understood, a person must also know what to say about our Sacraments . . . Baptism and the holy body and blood of Christ" (p. 358; LC Short Preface, 20). What is Luther trying to say? Is it enough to learn the Ten Commandments, or must we learn more? How are the commandments related to other topics, such as prayer and Baptism?

12. Luther writes, "It is the duty of every father of a family to question and examine his children and servants at least once a week and see what they know or are learning from the catechism" (p. 356; LC Short Preface, 4). If you could have a conversation with Luther about this statement, what would you say?

Sing

"Fear and Love Thy God and Lord," ELH 510

- *Lyrics*: B. Pedersen, tr. C. Døving, vv. 1–5; R. MacPherson, v. 6
- *Tune*: SPANISH CHANT (ELH 510; CW 124)
- *Alt. Tunes*: ST. GEORGE'S, WINDSOR (LBW 407; LSB 892; LW 88); SALZBURG (LHy 532)

1. Fear and love thy God and Lord,
   And revere His name and Word,
   Holy keep the Sabbath day,
   Honor to thy parents pay,
   Kill not, shun adultery,
   Steal not, lies and slander flee,
   Keep from covetousness free.
   Help me, Lord, I trust in Thee!

2. In the Father I believe,
   Who to all did being give,
   And in Jesus Christ, His Son,
   Who for all redemption won;
   And my faith I also place
   In the Holy Ghost, whose grace
   Sanctifies our souls and ways.
   Grant me faith through all my days!

3. Father, throned in heav'n above,
   Hallowed be Thy name in love;
   Let Thy kingdom come, we pray,
   And Thy will be done alway;
   Give us food, forgiveness send,
   In temptations aid extend,
   Save us, Lord, when comes our end!
   Amen! Lord, Thy Church defend!

4. God the Father, God the Son,
   God the Spirit, Three in One,
   I, baptized into Thy name,
   As Thy child Thy blessing claim;
   Grant that by Thy promised grace
   I my trust in Thee may place,
   All my sins with peace replace
   Till in heav'n I see Thy face.

5. Jesus, let my soul be fed
   With Thyself, the living Bread,
   For Thy flesh is meat indeed,
   And Thy cleansing blood I need;
   Let it cleanse from sin and shame,
   Keep me from all harm and blame,
   That Thy death I may proclaim,
   And forever bless Thy name!

6. To my pastor I confess
   All those sins which ache my breast.
   I acknowledge before him
   That I am entrapped in sin.
   From his lips I hear Thy Word
   As from Thine own lips 'twere heard.
   Thou proclaimest I'm forgiv'n.
   Freed by Thee to enter heav'n.

Remember

Martin Luther wrote his Small and Large Catechisms to assist pastors and parents in the Christian education of children. His catechisms were shorter and simpler than previous catechisms, because Luther wanted to focus on the basic doctrines of Scripture in a way that young children could easily comprehend and remember.

As summaries of God's Word, also containing many direct quotations from Holy Scripture, the catechisms bring to their readers the same blessings that God's Word offers. That is why Luther impressed upon fathers the importance of teaching the catechism in the home.

Lesson 2:
Trusting in and Calling upon God for Every Need

Pray

Lord God, heavenly Father, through Your Son You have promised us that whatever we ask in His name You will give us: We beseech You, keep us in Your Word, and grant us Your Holy Spirit, that He may govern us according to Your will; protect us from the power of the devil, from false doctrine and worship; and also defend our lives against all danger. Grant us Your blessing and peace, that we may in all things perceive Your merciful help, and both now and forever praise and glorify You as our gracious Father; through Your beloved Son, Jesus Christ, our Lord, who lives and reigns with You and the Holy Spirit, one true God, now and forever. Amen.

Veit Dietrich, Collect for the Sixth Sunday after Easter, in *ELH*, Collect #73, p. 156.

Read

- "The First Commandment," *Small Catechism* (pp. 316–17; SC I, 1–2)
- "The First Commandment," *Large Catechism* (pp. 359–61; LC I, 1–29)

Discuss

1. Sometimes people are not sure what counts as "religion." They may suppose that some individuals are more religious than others. Luther, however, says that everyone is religious, for everyone has a god. How does Luther define the meaning of the phrase "to have a god" (p. 359; LC I, 2, 10)?

---

2. In view of Luther's definition of "having a god," what does it mean to obey the First Commandment, in which the LORD says, "You shall have no other gods" but Him alone (pp. 360, 361; LC I, 13–16, 28)?

3. What does it mean to have an idol as one's god (p. 359–60; LC I, 5–12, 17–21)?

4. What is the worst form of idolatry (p. 360–61; LC I, 22–23)?

5. How should I properly view the connections between God, me, and the people from whom I receive God's blessings in this life (p. 361; LC I, 24–27)? *Note*: Here Luther introduces the concept of "vocation," which is a major theme of the Large Catechism.

6. Luther notes that God has attached two things to this commandment, one positive and one negative. What are they (p. 361; LC I, 29)? Note that these two themes are central threads to the Large Catechism's theological weave; expect to encounter them often.

Read

- "What Does God Say about All These Commandments?," *Small Catechism* (p. 327; SC I, 21–22)
- "Explanation of the Appendix of the First Commandment," *Large Catechism* (pp. 362–63; LC I, 30–48)

Discuss

7. Who may expect to receive the LORD's blessings under the First Commandment, and who should expect God's wrath instead (p. 362; LC I, 32–34)?

8. Luther concludes his discussion of the First Commandment by writing, "Where the heart is rightly set toward God and this commandment is observed, all the other commandments follow" (p. 363; LC I, 48). Explain why this is so. See Matthew 22:34–40; Hebrews 11:6.

Read

- "The Second Commandment," *Small Catechism* (p. 318; SC I, 3–4)
- "The Second Commandment," *Large Catechism* (pp. 363–67; LC I, 49–77)

Discuss

9. The First Commandment focuses on the heart; the Second Commandment focuses on something else—what is it (p. 364; LC I, 50)?

10. What are some ways in which God's name is misused (pp. 364–65; LC I, 51–62)? Apply these teachings to your life. See Matthew 15:8–9.

11. What are some ways in which God's name is properly used (pp. 365–66; LC I, 63–73)? Apply these teachings to your life. See Psalm 50:15.

12. How does Luther distinguish between a proper and improper use of God's name when making a solemn vow or oath (p. 366; LC I, 65–68)? Read Matthew 5:33–37; Matthew 26:59–61; 2 Corinthians 1:23; Galatians 1:20.

13. Luther concludes with some suggestions about how to teach the Second Commandment to children (pp. 366–67; LC I, 74–77). If you could have a conversation with Luther about those suggestions, what would you say?

14. Luther elsewhere makes two points clear: 1) no one except for Jesus Christ has ever kept God's commandments perfectly; and, 2) Jesus' perfect fulfillment of the Law becomes our righteousness by faith. How does this second point make the study of the Ten Commandments comforting to you? (It may help to review Question 7, above.)

Sing

"These Are the Holy Ten Commands," ELH 490, vv. 1–3, 12

- *Lyrics*: M. Luther, tr. ELH 490
- *Tune*: *IN GOTTES NAMEN FAHREN WIR* (ELH 490; CW 285; LSB 581; LW 331)
- *Alt. Tune*: *DIES SIND DIE HIEL'GEN* (TLH 287)

1. These are the holy Ten Commands
    Which God the Lord placed in our hands
    Through faithful Moses in the cloud
    On Sinai's mount, high and proud.
    Have mercy, Lord!

2. I am your only God and Lord;
    No other gods shall be adored.
    But you shall fully trust in Me
    With all your heart, loving me.
    Have mercy, Lord!

3. You shall not take in vain My name
    And bring upon yourself great shame;
    But you shall praise as right and true
    What I, your God, say and do.
    Have mercy, Lord!

12. Lord Jesus Christ, now help us all,
    Our Mediator from the Fall,
    Our works are all so full of sin,
    But You for us heav'n did win.
    Have mercy, Lord!

Remember

The *First Commandment* requires that we trust in the one true God for every need of body and soul; it commands faith. Since "without faith it is impossible to please God" (Hebrews 11:6), all other commandments are contained within the First Commandment.

The *Second Commandment* shifts our attention from our hearts toward our lips: when we trust God in our hearts, we will praise Him with our lips.

Both Scripture and human experience reveal that our hearts, and therefore our lips, are corrupt. Christ alone has fulfilled these commandments perfectly, and through faith His righteousness becomes ours.

LESSON 3:
Listening to God's Word and Honoring Parents

Pray

Lord God, heavenly Father, in mercy You have established the Christian home among us: We beseech You so to rule and direct our hearts, that we may be good examples to children and those subject to us, and not offend them by word or deed, but faithfully teach them to love Your Church and hear Your blessed Word. Give them Your Spirit and grace, that this seed may bring forth good fruit, so that our home life may advance Your glory, honor and praise, our own improvement and welfare, and give offense to no one; through the same, Your beloved Son, Jesus Christ, our Lord, who lives and reigns with You and the Holy Spirit, one true God, now and forever. Amen.

Veit Dietrich, Collect for the First Sunday after Epiphany, in *ELH*, Collect #21, pp. 149–50.

Read

- "The Third Commandment" (p. 319; SC I, 5–6)
- "The Third Commandment" (pp. 367–70; LC I, 78–102)

Discuss

1. What did this commandment mean in Old Testament times? See Genesis 2:3 and Exodus 20:8–11. How did some Jewish leaders misapply it in Christ's time? See Luke 6:1–11, 13:10–17, 14:1–6.

2. Luther claims that "this commandment . . . in its literal sense, does not apply to us Christians" (p. 368; LC I, 82). What does he mean by that? How does his view square with Colossians 2:16–17?

3. What two benefits does Luther identify in the Third Commandment (p. 368; LC I, 83–84)?

4. How often should the Third Commandment be obeyed— weekly? or daily? Explain (see p. 368; LC I, 89).

5. What makes a holy day holy (p. 369; LC I, 91–92)?

6. What three violations of this commandment does Luther identify (p. 369–70; LC I, 95–102)? Which of these do you see as most threatening to your spiritual life?

Read

- "The Fourth Commandment" (p. 320; SC I, 7–8)
- "The Fourth Commandment," first half (p. 370–75; LC I, 103–40)

Discuss

7. Which is higher—love or honor (p. 371; LC I, 105–7)? Explain.

8. In whose place do parents stand (p. 371; LC I, 108)? How does this truth make them worthy of honor (p. 372; LC I, 117)? Review the concept of "vocation," introduced in Lesson 2, Question 5.

9. Review Lesson 2, Question 6. How do the same themes of "threat" and "promise" apply in the Fourth Commandment (p. 374; LC I, 131–36)? See Ephesians 6:1–4.

Read

- "The Fourth Commandment," second half (p. 375–78; LC I, 141–78)

Discuss

10. What is the highest form of authority on this earth (p. 373; LC I, 126)? What is the source of all other earthly authority (p. 375; LC I, 141)?

11. Although the Fourth Commandment in its literal form requires that only one's "father and mother" be honored, Luther summarizes other portions of Scripture, as well as natural law, in identifying three other authorities who are entitled to similar respect. What are they, and why should they be honored, too (p. 375; LC I, 143, 150, 158)? See also Romans 13:1–7 and 1 Peter 5:5–6.

12. Scripture teaches that *spiritual* fatherhood is worthy of "double honor." In what specific ways does Luther recommend that laypeople should pay great respect to their pastors (p. 403; LC I, 161–63)? See 1 Timothy 5:17–20.

13. The Fourth Commandment explicitly requires that children honor their parents. Implicitly, it also indicates that parents should fulfill particular duties to their children (pp. 377–78; LC I, 167–68). Identify several of those duties, and emphasize the most important responsibility parents have. See Ephesians 6:4.

14. What distinction between faith and works does Luther identify (p. 375; LC I, 147)? See Romans 5:1–5, 6:1–4.

Sing

"These Are the Holy Ten Commands," ELH 490, vv. 1, 4, 5, 12

- *Lyrics*: M. Luther, tr. ELH 490
- *Tune*: IN GOTTES NAMEN FAHREN WIR (ELH 490; CW 285; LSB 581; LW 331)
- *Alt. Tune*: DIES SIND DIE HIEL'GEN (TLH 287)

1. These are the holy Ten Commands
   Which God the Lord placed in our hands
   Through faithful Moses in the cloud
   On Sinai's mount, high and proud.
   Have mercy, Lord!

4. You shall the day of rest keep free
   That you and yours may restful be
   As God from labor rested too.
   So now may He work in you.
   Have mercy, Lord!

5. You shall obey and gladly hear
   Your father and your mother dear;
   To them a helping hand to lend,
   As long as God life shall send.
   Have mercy, Lord!

12. Lord Jesus Christ, now help us all,
    Our Mediator from the Fall,
    Our works are all so full of sin,
    But You for us heav'n did win.
    Have mercy, Lord!

Remember

In the *Third Commandment*, God requires that we gather regularly to hear His Word. God wants us to do so because He intends to bless us through His Word with the comforting message that our sins are forgiven for Christ's sake. God does this both in the weekly divine service as well as on any other occasion that is made holy by the proper use of His Word, including daily home devotions.

In the *Fourth Commandment*, God requires that children honor their fathers and mothers as God's representatives on earth. By extension, this includes also the honor that people owe to teachers and government. God uses such offices as channels of His blessings to the people whom they serve. Therefore, the Fourth Commandment encompasses not only the duties children owe to their parents, or citizens to their government, but also the responsibilities of parents and civil magistrates to serve those whom God has entrusted to their care. In other words, the Fourth Commandment requires that each person live faithfully according to his or her *vocation*, whether as a son or daughter, a mother or a father, a citizen, or a civil ruler.

As we pray for God to grant us the ability to fulfill our vocations, we also recognize our many failures. We find comfort only in Christ, who obeyed every commandment on our behalf.

LESSON 4:
Protecting Lives and Safeguarding Marriages

Pray

Lord God, heavenly Father, we thank You, that by Your grace You have instituted holy matrimony, in which You keep us from unchastity and other offenses: We beseech You to send Your blessing upon every husband and wife, that they may not provoke each other to anger and strife, but live peaceably together in love and godliness, receive Your gracious help in all temptations, and raise their children in accordance with Your will. Grant that we all might walk before You in purity and holiness, put our trust in You, and lead such lives on earth, that in the world to come we may have everlasting life, through Your beloved Son, Jesus Christ, our Lord, who lives and reigns with You and the Holy Spirit, one true God, now and forever. Amen.

Veit Dietrich, Collect for the Second Sunday after Epiphany, in *ELH*, Collect #23, p. 150.

Read

- "The Fifth Commandment" (p. 321; SC I, 9–10)
- "The Fifth Commandment" (pp. 378–81; LC I, 179–98)

Discuss

1. Luther begins his discussion of the Fifth Commandment by saying that it does not apply to everyone (p. 379; LC I, 180–81). Whom does this commandment prohibit from harming or killing another person? Who, on the other hand, has the rightful authority to exercise corporal punishment or even to take another person's life? How does this distinction square with the discussion of "vocation" in Lesson 2, Question 5? See Proverbs 13:24, 22:15, 23:13–14; Romans 13:1–4.

2. What, in addition to physical murder, does this commandment prohibit (pp. 379–80; LC I, 182–88)?

3. Stated positively, what does this commandment require that people do for each other (p. 380; LC I, 189–92)?

4. In what sense does the Fifth Commandment flow naturally from the First Commandment (pp. 379, 380; LC I, 185, 187)?

5. Whom, especially, does God seek to protect by the Fifth Commandment (p. 381; LC I, 193–94). See Matthew 5:43–48.

6. What does Luther mean when he says that the Large Catechism's discussion of this commandment "would not be preaching for monks" (p. 381; LC I, 197)? See Matthew 23:27–28 and Isaiah 64:6 to understand Luther's biblical perspective more fully.

Read

- "The Sixth Commandment" (p. 322; SC I, 11–12)
- "The Sixth Commandment" (p. 381–84; LC I, 199–221)

Discuss

7. The Fifth Commandment protects a person's life. What does the Sixth Commandment protect (pp. 381–82; LC I, 200–1)?

8. Literally, the Sixth Commandment forbids "adultery," that is, a husband or wife having sexual relations with someone other than his or her spouse. What explanation does Luther give for the narrow focus of this commandment in Old Testament times, and what justification does he offer for applying the commandment more broadly to include "all kinds of unchastity" (p. 382; LC I, 201–5)?

9. What special blessings does God seek to protect by the Sixth Commandment (pp. 382–83; LC I, 206–10)? See Genesis 1:27–28; Psalm 128; Proverbs 22:6; Ephesians 5:33, and 6:4.

10. Luther lived during a time when church authorities tended to view the celibacy of priests and nuns as superior to married life. How does Luther apply Genesis 1:27–28 and 1 Corinthians 7:1–9 to show the folly of exalting celibacy above marriage (p. 383; LC I, 211–16)? Does this mean that no one is ever called by God to be celibate? See Mathew 19:11–12.

11. What duties does Luther identify for pastors, parents, and civil government with respect to marriage and the education of children (p. 383; LC I, 217–18)?

12. On the one hand, the sinful nature resists chastity (p. 383; LC I, 215). On the other hand, Luther says that Christians can learn to live under the Spirit's guidance in such a way that "chastity will follow [naturally] without any command" (p. 384; LC I, 219). How do these two statements fit together? Compare also Luther's comment about "where nature runs its course"—is he speaking in that instance of human nature as God created it, or of the fallen, sinful human nature (p. 383; LC I, 212)?

Sing

"These Are the Holy Ten Commands," ELH 490, vv. 1, 6, 7, 12

- *Lyrics*: M. Luther, tr. ELH 490
- *Tune*: IN GOTTES NAMEN FAHREN WIR (ELH 490; CW 285; LSB 581; LW 331)
- *Alt. Tune*: DIES SIND DIE HIEL'GEN (TLH 287)

1. These are the holy Ten Commands
    Which God the Lord placed in our hands
    Through faithful Moses in the cloud
    On Sinai's mount, high and proud.
    Have mercy, Lord!

6. You shall not in great anger kill,
    Nor vengeance, neither hatred feel.
    With patience and with quiet mood,
    E'en to your foe, do what's good.
    Have mercy, Lord!

7. Be faithful to your marriage vows,
    Your heart give only to your spouse,
    And keep your life with chastity;
    So faithful and modest be.
    Have mercy, Lord!

12. Lord Jesus Christ, now help us all,
    Our Mediator from the Fall,
    Our works are all so full of sin,
    But You for us heav'n did win.
    Have mercy, Lord!

Remember

God has issued the Ten Commandments out of love. As our loving Father, He seeks to protect people's lives by the *Fifth Commandment*. That commandment forbids any thought, word, or action that would harm our neighbor, and requires that our thoughts, words, and actions promote our neighbor's physical well-being. Civil government, however, may rightfully act as God's representative on earth to punish a capital offender by execution. Aside from that special circumstance, of course, civil government should promote and defend its citizens' lives, just as all citizens also should do according to their vocations.

In the *Sixth Commandment*, God protects marriage and the family. God created us male and female and instituted marriage as the proper vocation for the one-flesh union. Marriage, therefore, is the divinely established vocation for bearing and raising children. Although God calls some people to a vocation of life-long celibacy, no one has the authority to forbid marriage, nor should anyone claim that those who remain celibate are holier than those who marry. Whether married or not, all people have a responsibility to promote chastity and defend marriage through their thoughts, words, and actions.

The only perfect spouse is Jesus Christ, who "loved the church and gave Himself up for her, that He might sanctify and cleanse her with the washing of water by the word" (Ephesians 5:25–26). He provides not only the model for all earthly marriages (vv. 22–33), but also the remedy for our sins by which we endanger marriages. "Blessed are those who are called to the marriage supper of the Lamb!" (Revelation 19:9).

LESSON 5:
Respecting People's Property and Honor

Pray

O Lord God, heavenly Father: You are merciful, and through Christ promised us that You will neither judge nor condemn us, but graciously forgive us all our sins, and abundantly provide for all our wants of body and soul: We pray that by Your Holy Spirit You would establish in our hearts a confident faith in Your mercy, and teach us also to be merciful to our neighbor, that we may not judge or condemn others, but willingly forgive all, and, judging only ourselves, lead blessed lives in Your fear; through Your beloved Son, Jesus Christ, our Lord, who lives and reigns with You and the Holy Spirit, one true God, now and forever. Amen.

Veit Dietrich, Collect for the Fourth Sunday after Trinity, in *ELH*, Collect #89, p. 159.

Read

- "The Seventh Commandment" (p. 323; SC I, 13–14)
- "The Seventh Commandment" (pp. 384–88; LC I, 222–53)

Discuss

1. How does Luther define stealing (p. 384; LC I, 224)? Aside from the obvious thieves, who else is guilty of stealing, and how so (pp. 384–85; LC I, 225–30)? Against which of these "hidden" violations of the Seventh Commandment must you be especially careful to guard yourself in your vocation?

2. What, then, does the Seventh Commandment require (p. 385; LC I, 233)? See Deuteronomy 22:1–4.

3. What warnings should be sounded against those who steal, whether through open thievery or hidden trickery (pp. 385–86; LC I, 231–39)?

4. How does God punish people in this life for their acts of stealing (pp. 386–87; LC I, 240–46)? See Luke 12:16–21; Matthew 6:19–21; James 1:9–11.

5. How should common people respond to those who steal from them (pp. 386–87; LC I, 240–46)? See Matthew 6:12; Psalm 37:25. How do the vocations of pastor and civil magistrate differ with respect to their treatment of thieves (p. 387; LC I, 248–49)?

6. What would the Seventh Commandment have us to do for our neighbors in need (pp. 387–88; LC I, 247, 250–53)? See Proverbs 19:17; Matthew 5:42; Galatians 6:6–10.

Read

*   "The Eighth Commandment" (p. 324; SC I, 15–16)
*   "The Eighth Commandment" (pp. 388–92; LC I, 254–91)

Discuss

7. What does God protect by the Eighth Commandment (pp. 388, 392; LC I, 256, 285–91)?

8. How does this commandment apply to the vocations of witnesses and judges in a court of law (p. 388; LC I, 257–61)? See Deuteronomy 19:15–21; 1 Kings 3:28; Proverbs 17:23, 29:4; Isaiah 5:20.

9. Why is a pastor's reputation especially important to protect (p. 389; LC I, 262)? Review Lesson 2, Questions 9–12 concerning the Second Commandment.

10. How does the Eighth Commandment apply to the vocations of common people (p. 389; LC I, 263–65)?

11. Why does Luther think a person must distinguish properly between "judging sin" and "knowing sin" in order to understand this commandment (pp. 389–90; LC I, 265–73)?

12. When does someone have not only the permission but in fact the responsibility to rebuke, rather than remain silent about, someone's sin (pp. 390–91; LC I, 274–83)? Explain how the correct answer to this question varies according to a person's vocation as a civil magistrate, a pastor, or a Christian friend. See Ezekiel 33:1–9; Matthew 18:15–18; Luke 17:3–4; John 3:19–21; James 5:19–20.

13. Under what circumstances must a sin be rebuked publicly, and why (p. 391; LC I, 284)?

Sing

"These Are the Holy Ten Commands," ELH 490, vv. 1, 8, 9, 12

- *Lyrics*: M. Luther, tr. ELH 490
- *Tune*: *IN GOTTES NAMEN FAHREN WIR* (ELH 490; CW 285; LSB 581; LW 331)
- *Alt. Tune*: *DIES SIND DIE HIEL'GEN* (TLH 287)

1. These are the holy Ten Commands
   Which God the Lord placed in our hands
   Through faithful Moses in the cloud
   On Sinai's mount, high and proud.
   Have mercy, Lord!

8. You shall not steal one's gold or goods,
   Nor rob another's sweat and blood,
   But to the poor in ev'ry land
   Be giving with open hand.
   Have mercy, Lord!

9. And you shall not false witness bear,
   Nor lie nor cheat your neighbor e'er.
   Excuse him and speak well of him,
   The best in all see in him.
   Have mercy, Lord!

12. Lord Jesus Christ, now help us all,
    Our Mediator from the Fall,
    Our works are all so full of sin,
    But You for us heav'n did win.
    Have mercy, Lord!

Remember

The *Seventh Commandment* protects personal property, but not merely against open thievery. God here also forbids laziness, carelessness, or other attitudes and behaviors that diminish the value of our neighbor's goods and means of making a living. Rather than thinking we have achieved spiritual perfection by not openly robbing from our neighbor, we should humbly confess our secret violations of this commandment, asking Christ to forgive us.

The *Eighth Commandment* protects personal honor. Everyone has a responsibility toward his neighbor in this regard, according to his or her particular vocation. God even wants the honor of dishonorable people to be protected as best as possible. Therefore, Christian friends and pastors should rebuke sins privately. However, when a sin becomes publicly known, then the church must testify publicly against it, lest the weak be misled into thinking that what is evil is good. Similarly, courts of law must exercise justice publicly. Aside from these special occasions, a person's tongue should be carefully controlled, letting the silence of forgiveness cover a multitude of sins.

"Neither do I condemn you," says Jesus. "Go and sin no more" (John 8:11).

LESSON 6:
Serving in the Roles God Assigns

Pray

Lord God, heavenly Father, You have bountifully given Your blessing and our daily bread: We beseech You, preserve us from covetousness, and so enliven our hearts that we willingly share Your blessed gifts with our needy brethren; that we may be found faithful stewards of Your gifts, and abide in Your grace when we shall be removed from our stewardship, and shall come before Your judgment, through Your beloved Son, Jesus Christ, our Lord, who lives and reigns with You and the Holy Spirit, one true God, now and forever. Amen.

Veit Dietrich, Collect for the Ninth Sunday after Trinity, in *ELH*, Collect #99, p. 160.

Read

- "The Ninth Commandment" (p. 325; SC I, 17–18)
- "The Tenth Commandment" (p. 326; SC I, 19–20)
- "The Ninth and Tenth Commandments" (pp. 392–95; LC I, 292–310)

Discuss

1. How have you previously understood the word "covet"? Compare your definition to the meaning Luther draws from Scripture and summarizes in his discussion of the Ninth and Tenth Commandments (p. 394; LC I, 307). See Psalm 119:36–37; Proverbs 21:25–26; Matthew 5:8.

2. Why does Luther claim that the literal sense of the Tenth Commandment is limited to the Jews of the Old Testament (pp. 392–93; LC I, 293–95)? What broader sense does Luther identify as applying to people of all time (p. 393; LC I, 296)?

3. Luther suggests that the Seventh Commandment applies to the common people, and the Ninth and Tenth Commandments apply to lawyers and judges (p. 393–94; LC I, 299–302). Why does he make this distinction?

4. Even if the Ninth and Tenth Commandments apply especially to lawyers and judges, how do they apply also to common people (p. 393–95; LC I, 297–98, 303–4, 307–10)?

5. Review Luther's description of how people in Bible times stole a man's wife from him (p. 394; LC I, 305–6). See also Mark 6:17–20, 10:9. What techniques are prevalent today for shifting a wife's loyalty away from her husband, or a husband's loyalty away from his wife? How can Christians protect marriages in view of the Tenth Commandment?

6. Contemplate the following statement: "Some women are so busy working for other people that they aren't able to help in their own family as they should. When this happens it is because someone is breaking the Tenth Commandment. It is not always easy to show who is at fault in such a case" (Nils C. Oesleby, "The Distinction between the Sixth, Seventh, Ninth, [and] Tenth Commandments," *Lutheran Sentinel*, 9 May 1963, 138–40, at 139). Read Titus 2:1–5. What blessings in verses 4–5 does the Tenth Commandment protect? What hinders Christians from applying the Tenth Commandment in this manner today?

Read

- "Conclusion of the Ten Commandments" (pp. 395–98; LC I, 311–33)

Discuss

7. Luther states bluntly that "apart from the Ten Commandments no work or thing can be good or pleasing to God" (p. 395; LC I, 311). Against whom was he speaking?

8. Consider how Luther again emphasizes the importance of vocation when stating that the Ten Commandments are "common, everyday, household works that one neighbor can do for another" (p. 395; LC I, 313). He applies the principle of vocation specifically to a simple girl caring for a child (p. 396; LC I, 314). Apply it now to your own life, too.

9. Luther writes, "No person can go far enough to keep one of the Ten Commandments as it should be kept" (p. 396; LC I, 316). Select any two commandments, review what they require, and indicate how your own life has fallen short of God's perfect standard.

10. The core of holiness is expressed in the First Commandment; the starting point for any sin, similarly, is a violation of the First Commandment. Review the meaning of the First Commandment (p. 307; LC I, 324–25). Then summarize how Luther locates the Second through Fifth Commandments in the First Commandment (p. 397; LC I, 326–29).

11. Luther emphasizes once more that the commandments include "both an angry, threatening word and a friendly promise" (p. 396; LC I, 322; see also p. 397; LC I, 323). As for the friendly promise, Luther writes that "the Apostles' Creed and the Lord's Prayer must come to our aid" (p. 396; LC I, 316). What comfort can sinners find in those two sources?

12. Always the educator, Luther concludes with an exhortation that pastors and parents teach God's Word to the young (p. 398; LC I, 330–33). Identify the most significant lessons you have learned during this study of the Ten Commandments from Luther's Large Catechism. Then write a plan for sharing those insights with the people whom God has entrusted to your care.

Sing

"These Are the Holy Ten Commands," ELH 490, vv. 1, 10–12

- *Lyrics*: M. Luther, tr. ELH 490
- *Tune*: *IN GOTTES NAMEN FAHREN WIR* (ELH 490; CW 298; LSB 581; LW 331)
- *Alt. Tune*: *DIES SIND DIE HIEL'GEN* (TLH 287)

1. These are the holy Ten Commands
    Which God the Lord placed in our hands
    Through faithful Moses in the cloud
    On Sinai's mount, high and proud.
    Have mercy, Lord!

10. You shall your neighbor's spouse and home
    Not seek nor covet for your own;
    But you shall wish them ev'ry good,
    As your own heart for you would.
    Have mercy, Lord!

11. To us God gave these Ten Commands
    That you might learn, O child of man,
    Your sinfulness and also know
    To live for God, as you go.
    Have mercy, Lord!

12. Lord Jesus Christ, now help us all,
    Our Mediator from the Fall,
    Our works are all so full of sin,
    But You for us heav'n did win.
    Have mercy, Lord!

Remember

The *Ninth* and *Tenth Commandments* identify holiness primarily as a concern of the heart. It is not enough to avoid open stealing (by obeying the Seventh Commandment outwardly) or to avoid open adultery (by obeying the Sixth Commandment outwardly). God also forbids coveting, and in its place He commands genuine love for our neighbor in all circumstances. In this manner, all of the commandments ultimately may be found within the First Commandment: that we fear God, trust God, and love God above all else, for out of such a heart naturally flows service to our neighbor.

After studying the Ten Commandments, it becomes clear that our theology cannot end here. The Ten Commandments reveal a disturbing gap between God's holiness and our own wicked thoughts, words, and actions. To study the Ten Commandments alone, we would be left with God's threatened wrath overshadowing His promised salvation. Luther therefore directs us back to the whole of Scripture, where we find not only the Law that convicts us of sin, but also the Gospel that reveals our Savior, Jesus Christ. The remainder of Luther's Large Catechism focuses on that comforting Gospel of forgiveness, as encapsulated in the Apostles' Creed, the Lord's Prayer, Holy Baptism, and the Lord's Supper.

Worshiping One God in Trinity and the Trinity in Unity

Pray

O Lord God, heavenly Father: We poor sinners confess that in our flesh dwells no good thing, and that, left to ourselves, we die and perish in sin, since that which is born of flesh is flesh and cannot see the kingdom of God. But we pray that You would grant us Your grace and mercy, and for the sake of Your Son, Jesus Christ, send Your Holy Spirit into our hearts, that being regenerate we may firmly believe the forgiveness of sins according to Your promise in baptism, and that we may daily increase in Christian love and in other good works, until we at last obtain eternal salvation; through the same Your beloved Son Jesus Christ, our Lord, who lives and reigns with You and the Holy Spirit, one true God, now and forever. Amen.

Veit Dietrich, Collect for Trinity Sunday, in *ELH*, Collect #81, p. 157–58.

Read

- "The Apostles' Creed," *Large Catechism* (pp. 398–99; LC II, 1–8, 63–70)

Discuss

1. Contrast the Apostles' Creed with the Ten Commandments, both as to their main messages as well as to the ways in which God has made those messages known (pp. 398, 406; LC II, 1, 67–69). See Romans 2:14–15; Romans 3:21–26; 1 Corinthians 2:12.

2. Previous teachers in the church had divided the Apostles' Creed into twelve phrases. Luther, by contrast, taught the Creed in three articles. Why three and not some other number (p. 399; LC II, 5–8)? See Matthew 28:19–20.

Read

- "The First Article," *Small Catechism* (p. 328; SC II, 1–2)
- "Article I," *Large Catechism* (pp. 399–401; LC II, 9–24)

Discuss

3. How does the First Article of the Creed relate to the First Commandment (pp. 399, 400–1; LC II, 10–11, 19–24)?

4. What has God the Father done for us, and what does He continue to do for us even today (p. 400; LC II, 13–18)? See Genesis 1:26–28; Matthew 6:11,25–34.

Read

- "The Second Article," *Small Catechism* (p. 329; SC II, 3–4)
- "The Apostles' Creed," *Large Catechism*, Article II (pp. 401–2; LC II, 25–33)

Discuss

5. Luther reduces the Second Article to one brief phrase, "In Jesus Christ, our Lord." Explain how the word "lord" summarizes everything else mentioned in the Second Article (pp. 401, 402; LC II, 26–27, 31–32). See John 20:26–29.

6. How is it that Christ is the kind of lord who can save all people (pp. 401–2; LC II, 28–30)? See Romans 5:12–21; Revelation 17:14, 19:16.

7. It may seem surprising that Luther devoted so little space in his Large Catechism to the Second Article. We know from elsewhere in the Large Catechism, plus his other writings, that Luther considered the truths confessed in the Second Article to be of the utmost importance. Why do you suppose he treated them so briefly here?

Read

- "The Third Article," *Small Catechism* (p. 330; SC II, 5–6)
- "Article III," *Large Catechism* (pp. 402–8; LC II, 34–62)

Discuss

8. Luther notes that the Bible refers to many types of spirits. What is unique about the Holy Spirit (p. 403; LC II, 35–36)? See Luke 7:21; 1 Corinthians 2:11; Hebrews 12:22–24; 1 John 4:1–2.

9. If we are saved by Christ alone, then why is preaching necessary (pp. 403–4; LC II, 37–45)? See Romans 10:14.

10. Sometimes the words "church" and "congregation" mean the same thing; sometimes they mean different things. The same confusion occurs in our English that occurred Luther's German. How does Luther use terms such as "gathering" and "congregation" to explain the proper meaning of "the communion of saints" (pp. 404–5; LC II, 47–53)? See Ephesians 1:22–23, 4:4–16.

11. Through what means does the Holy Spirit bestow upon a gathering of believers the benefits of salvation that Christ attained for them (pp. 403, 405; LC II, 38, 54–56)? See Matthew 26:26–28; John 20:21–23; Acts 2:38; 1 John 5:7–8.

12. Why does Luther claim that "we are only half pure and holy" (pp. 405–6; LC II, 57–60)? See Romans 7:14–25; 1 Corinthians 13:9–12, 15:35–54.

Sing:

"We All Believe in One True God," ELH 38

- *Lyrics*: M. Luther, tr. composite, ELH 38
- *Tune*: *WIR GLAUBEN ALL* (ELH 38; CW 271; LBW 374; LHy 71; LSB 954; LW 213; TLH 251)

1. We all believe in one true God,
   Who created earth and heaven,
   The Father, who to us in love
   Hath the right of children given.
   He both soul and body feedeth,
   All we need He doth provide us.
   He through snares and perils leadeth,
   Watching that no harm betide us.
   He careth for us day and night;
   All things are governed by His might.

2. We all believe in Jesus Christ,
   His own Son, our Lord, possessing
   An equal Godhead, throne, and might,
   Source of ev'ry grace and blessing.
   Born of Mary, virgin mother,
   By the power of the Spirit,
   Made true man, our elder Brother,
   That the lost might life inherit,
   Was crucified for sinful men
   And raised by God to life again.

3. We all confess the Holy Ghost,
   Who sweet grace and comfort giveth
   And with the Father and the Son
   In eternal glory liveth,
   Who the Church, His own creation,
   Keeps in unity of spirit;
   Here forgiveness and salvation
   Daily come through Jesus' merit.
   All flesh shall rise, and we shall be
   In bliss with God eternally.

Remember

The Apostles' Creed assists Christians in passing on the one true faith to future generations, since it provides a clear and concise summary of what Holy Scripture reveals about God. Mysteriously, God is three Persons in one Godhead. This Triune God provides for all our needs of body and soul. Although the three Persons work together, we particularly acknowledge God the Father as our Creator and Preserver, God the Son as our Redeemer and Lord, and God the Holy Spirit as our Sanctifier and Comforter.

Two words within the Creed deserve special attention, since they can so easily be misunderstood. First, in calling Jesus Christ our "Lord" we do not primarily have in mind that we owe our obedience to Him (although that also is true). Rather, we especially wish to emphasize that Christ is our great protector who has defeated Satan on our behalf and continues to keep us safe for all eternity. Second, in speaking of the Christian "church" we do not primarily have in mind the external institution, but rather the gathering of people's hearts around the Word and Sacraments, through which means the Holy Spirit creates and strengthens their faith in Jesus Christ as the one true Savior.

Praising God through Prayer

Pray

O Jesus Christ, almighty Son of God, You are no longer in humiliation here on earth, but are seated at the right hand of Your Father, Lord over all things: We beseech You, send us Your Holy Spirit; give Your Church pious pastors, preserve Your Word, control and restrain the devil and all who would oppress us; mightily uphold Your kingdom, until all Your enemies have been put under Your feet, that we may hold the victory over sin, death, and the devil; through You, who live and reign with God the Father and the Holy Spirit, one true God, now and forever. Amen.

Veit Dietrich, Collect for the Ascension of Our Lord, in *ELH*, Collect #75, p. 157.

Read

* "The Lord's Prayer," *Small Catechism* (p. 331; SC III, 1–2)
* "The Lord's Prayer," *Large Catechism* (pp. 408–12; LC II, 1–34)

Discuss

1. Luther notes that prayer is highly important. What did Jesus do to ensure that people would know how to pray (pp. 408, 410–11; LC III, 1–3, 22–23)? See Luke 11:1–4.

2. How does prayer fit with the Second Commandment (pp. 408–9; LC III, 4–8)? See Psalm 50:15; Matthew 6:5,7.

3. How does Luther's discussion of the Fourth Commandment shed light on the significance of prayer (pp. 409–10; LC III, 9–13)? See Luke 11:9–13 for another analogy.

4. What makes a person worthy to pray? In what sense can even the lowliest of Christians claim just as much right to pray as St. Peter or St. Paul (p. 410; LC III, 14–16)? See Matthew 8:8.

5. Luther suggests that three considerations should motivate a person to pray. What are they (pp. 408, 410–11; LC III, 5, 17–21, 22–24)? See 1 Thessalonians 5:17–18; John 14:13–14.

6. And what pitfalls must one avoid when it comes to prayer (pp. 411–12, LC III, 25–27, 33)? See Psalm 51:17; Matthew 6:5,7; Luke 18:9–14.

7. Why is daily prayer important (pp. 411–12; LC III, 26–32)? See Ephesians 6:10–18.

Read

- "The First Petition," *Small Catechism* (p. 332; SC III, 3–5)
- "The First Petition," *Large Catechism* (pp. 412–13; LC III, 35–48)

Discuss

8. In what way does the First Petition pray for what God commands in the Second Commandment (pp. 412–13; LC III, 39–46)?

9. Why is it important to have in mind both worldly people and Christians when praying the First Petition (pp. 413; LC III, 47–48)?

Read

- "The Second Petition," *Small Catechism* (p. 333; SC III, 6–8)
- "The Second Petition," *Large Catechism* (pp. 413–15; LC III, 49–58)

Discuss

10. How does the Second Petition relate to the Apostles' Creed (pp. 414; LC III, 51, 54)?

11. To which two groups of people, and during which two periods of time, does Luther apply this evangelism prayer (p. 414; LC III, 53)?

12. What is the point of Luther's illustration concerning the rich emperor and the poor beggar (p. 415; LC III, 57–58)?

Sing

"Our Father, Thou in Heaven Above," ELH 383, vv. 1–3, 9

- *Lyrics*: M. Luther, tr. C. Winkworth, ELH 383
- *Tune*: *VATER UNSER* (ELH 383; CW 410; LBW 310; LHy 359; LSB 766; LW 431; TLH 458)

1. Our Father, Thou in heav'n above,
    Who biddest us to dwell in love
    As brethren of one family
    And cry for all we need to Thee;
    Teach us to mean the words we say,
    And from the inmost heart to pray.

2. All hallowed be Thy name, O Lord!
    O let us firmly keep Thy word,
    And lead, according to Thy name,
    A holy life, untouched by blame;
    Let no false teachings do us hurt;
    All poor deluded souls convert.

3. Thy kingdom come! Thine let it be
    In time and through eternity!
    O let Thy Holy Spirit dwell
    With us, to rule and guide us well;
    From Satan's mighty pow'r and rage
    Preserve Thy Church from age to age.

(*continued on next page*)

9. Amen! That is, so let it be!
   Strengthen our faith and trust in Thee
   That we may doubt not, but believe
   That what we ask we shall receive.
   Thus in Thy name and at Thy word
   We say, "Amen. Now hear us, Lord."

Lyrics are in the public domain.

Remember

In the Bible we find God's command that we should pray, His promise to hear our prayer, and many examples of how to pray—including the model prayer, known as the Lord's Prayer. We approach God's throne of grace confidently, not because we find any worthiness in ourselves but solely because God graciously invites us to call upon Him, as our Heavenly Father (*Introduction or Address to the Lord's Prayer*). Through prayer, we rightfully use God's name, and through prayer we ask that God's name be used properly among us (*Second Commandment* and *First Petition*). Our prayers are meditations upon the summary of doctrine contained in the Apostles' Creed. For example, we ask that "God's Kingdom come," which means that Christ our Lord would destroy the devil's work in our lives and that the Holy Spirit would daily forgive our sins through the Means of Grace (*Second Petition; cf. Second* and *Third Articles*).

LESSON 9:
Praying to God for All Our Needs

Pray

Lord God, heavenly Father, in the wilderness by Your Son You abundantly fed four thousand men, besides women and children, with seven loaves and a few small fish: We beseech You, graciously abide among us with Your blessing, and keep us from covetousness and the cares of this life, that we may seek first Your kingdom and Your righteousness, and in all things needed for body and soul, experience Your ever-present help; through Your Son, our Lord Jesus Christ, who lives and reigns with you and the Holy Spirit, one true God, now and forever. Amen.

Veit Dietrich, Collect for the Seventh Sunday after Trinity, in *ELH*, Collect #95, p. 160.

Read

- "The Third Petition," *Small Catechism* (p. 334; SC III, 9–11)
- "The Third Petition," *Large Catechism* (pp. 415–17; LC III, 59–70)

Discuss

1. By what devices does the devil seek to thwart God's will in our lives (pp. 415–16; LC III, 62–66)? See Matthew 7:15; 2 Corinthians 2:10–11; 1 Timothy 3:1–7; 1 Peter 5:6–9.

2. What confidence ought we have as we pray the Third Petition (p. 416; LC III, 67–70)? See John 16:33; 1 John 4:4, 5:4–5.

Read

- "The Fourth Petition," *Small Catechism* (p. 335; SC III, 12–14)
- "The Fourth Petition," *Large Catechism* (pp. 417–18; LC III, 71–84)

Discuss

3. What does a Christian's prayer for "daily bread" include (pp. 417–18; LC III, 72, 76–81)?

4. How does the Fourth Petition flow naturally from the First and Second Commandments, and the First Article (pp. 417, 418; LC III, 72, 82–84)?

5. What relationship does Luther discover between the Fourth Petition and the Fourth Commandment (p. 417; LC III, 73–75? How does this fit with the doctrine of vocation, which was introduced in Lesson 2, Question 5?

Read

- "The Fifth Petition," *Small Catechism* (p. 336; SC III, 15–16)
- "The Fifth Petition," *Large Catechism* (pp. 418–20; LC III, 85–98)

Discuss

6. What three influences cause us to sin daily (p. 419; LC III, 86–89)? See 1 Peter 5:8; Proverbs 1:10; Galatians 5:17.

7. If God forgives us even before we ask, then why should we nonetheless pray for His forgiveness (p. 419; LC, 88, 92)?

8. If God forgives us even before we forgive others, then why does the Fifth Petition include the phrase, "as we forgive those who trespass against us" (pp. 419–20; LC III, 93–98)? See Matthew 18:21–35.

Read

- "The Sixth Petition," *Small Catechism* (p. 337; SC III, 15–16)
- "The Sixth Petition," *Large Catechism* (pp. 420–21; LC III, 99–111)

Discuss

9. What three sources of temptation does Luther identify, and how might these operate in different degrees for different stages of life (p. 420–21; LC III, 100–4, 107–8)? How, in particular, is the devil dangerous (p. 421; LC III, 111)? See Genesis 3:1–4; Revelation 12:9.

10. What is the difference between temptation and sin (p. 421; LC III, 106–8)? See 1 Corinthians 10:11–13; 2 Timothy 2:3.

11. What comfort is found in Christ's instruction to pray the Sixth Petition (p. 421; LC, 106, 111)?

Read

- "The Seventh Petition," *Small Catechism* (p. 338; SC III, 19–21)
- "The Seventh Petition," *Large Catechism* (pp. 421–23; LC III, 112–24)

Discuss

12. Explain the difference between being delivered "from evil" and "from the evil one," noting why each of these is important (p. 422; LC III, 113–16).

13. What does "Amen" mean, and why is it an appropriate conclusion to a prayer (pp. 422–23; LC III, 119–24)? See 2 Corinthians 1:18–22; Titus 1:1–3; James 1:6–8.

Sing

"Our Father, Thou in Heaven Above," ELH 383, vv. 4–9

- *Lyrics*: M. Luther, tr. C. Winkworth, ELH 383
- *Tune*: *VATER UNSER* (ELH 383; CW 410; LBW 310; LHy 359; LSB 766; LW 431; TLH 458)

4. Thy will be done on earth, O Lord,
   As where in heav'n Thou art adored!
   Patience in time of grief bestow,
   Obedience true in weal and woe;
   Our sinful flesh and blood control
   That thwart Thy will within the soul.

5. Give us this day our daily bread,
   Let us be duly clothed and fed;
   And keep Thou from our homes afar
   Famine and pestilence and war,
   That we may live in godly peace
   Unvexed by cares and avarice.

6. Forgive our sins, that they no more
   May grieve and haunt us as before,
   As we forgive their trespasses
   Who unto us have done amiss;
   Thus let us dwell in charity
   And serve each other willingly.

7. Into temptation lead us not,
   And when the foe doth war and plot
   Against our souls on ev'ry hand,
   Then armed with faith, O may we stand
   Against him as a valiant host
   Through comfort of the Holy Ghost.

8. Deliv'rance from all evil give,
   For yet in evil days we live.
   Redeem us from eternal death,
   And, when we yield our dying breath,
   Console us, grant us calm release,
   And take our souls to Thee in peace.

9. Amen! That is, so let it be!
   Strengthen our faith and trust in Thee
   That we may doubt not, but believe
   That what we ask we shall receive.
   Thus in Thy name and at Thy word
   We say, "Amen. Now hear us, Lord."

Lyrics are in the public domain.

Remember

Satan would have us doubt that God cares for us or provides for us. In prayer, we direct our hearts back to God, clinging to His Word in faith. God has promised to supply our every need, both of body and soul, and so we ask this of Him in prayer. The Lord's Prayer instructs us to seek God's will for our lives, not our own plans (*Third Petition*); to trust in the Lord for all of our needs on this earth (*Fourth Petition*); to turn to the Lord for His forgiveness for our sins, and to turn to our neighbor to share that forgiveness when we have been sinned against (*Fifth Petition*); to flee to God, as to a mighty fortress, in times of temptation (*Sixth Petition*); and, to trust that God our Savior will deliver us at last from every evil of body and soul, and even from Satan himself (*Seventh Petition*). All of this we can ask, on the basis of God's own promise and invitation, with full confidence. Amen!

LESSON 10:
Becoming God's Child through Holy Baptism

Pray

Lord God, heavenly Father, You manifested Yourself, with the Holy Spirit, in the fullness of grace at the baptism of Your dear Son, and with Your voice directed us to Him who has borne our sins, that we might receive grace and the remission of sins: Keep us, we beseech You, in the true faith; and inasmuch as we have been baptized in accordance with Your command, and the example of Your dear Son, we pray You to strengthen our faith by Your Holy Spirit, and lead us to everlasting life and salvation; through Your beloved Son, Jesus Christ, our Lord, who lives and reigns with You and the Holy Spirit, one true God, now and forever. Amen.

Veit Dietrich, Collect for the Baptism of Our Lord, in *ELH*, Collect #38, p. 152.

Read

- "Baptism: First," *Small Catechism* (p. 339; SC IV, 1–4)
- "Baptism," *Large Catechism* (pp. 423–25; LC IV, 1–22)

Discuss

1. Who "invented" Baptism, and with which words of institution (p. 423; LC IV, 3–6)? See Matthew 28:19–20; Mark 16:16.

2. Whose work is Baptism, and by whom is a person baptized (p. 424; LC IV, 10–13)? See Colossians 2:11–12; Titus 3:4–7.

3. What does Luther mean when calling Baptism "divine water," and how does he refute people who claim Baptism is merely water, powerless to accomplish any spiritual effect (p. 424–25; LC IV, 14–18, 22)?

4. In what respects is God's institution of Baptism comparable to God's institution of parenthood (p. 425; LC IV, 19–21)?

Read

- "Baptism: Second," *Small Catechism* (p. 339; SC IV, 5–8)
- "Baptism," *Large Catechism*, continued (pp. 425–26; LC IV, 23–31)

Discuss

5. For what purpose did God establish Baptism (pp. 425–26; LC IV, 23–27)? See Mark 16:16; Matthew 28:19–20; Acts 2:38.

6. To claim that "Baptism saves you" may seem to deny that we are saved by faith alone. How does Luther resolve this confusion (p. 426; LC IV, 28–31)? See Romans 3:28; 1 Peter 3:21.

Read

- "Baptism: Third," *Small Catechism* (p. 340; SC IV, 9–10)
- "Baptism," *Large Catechism*, continued (pp. 426–28; LC IV, 32–46)

Discuss

7. Who receives the benefits of Baptism, and how (pp. 426–27; LC IV, 32–36)?

8. The preceding points merit careful attention and frequent repetition, since heterodox teachers circulate so many false opinions concerning Baptism. Once again, whose work is Baptism, and what does that work accomplish (p. 427; LC IV, 37–46)? See John 3:5; Acts 2:38, 22:16; Romans 6:3–4; 1 Corinthians 6:11; Ephesians 5:25–27; Titus 3:4–7.

Read

- "Baptism," *Large Catechism*, continued (pp. 428–29; LC IV, 47–63)

Discuss

9. The rejection of infant Baptism was new in Luther's day; for the first 1500 years of church history, infant Baptism had rarely been questioned. What argument does Luther offer to demonstrate that infant Baptism pleases God (p. 428; LC IV, 47–51)? See Matthew 18:1–6; Luke 1:39–41.

10. Is Baptism still valid and helpful if a person does not have faith (pp. 428–29; LC IV, 52–63)? See, for an analogy concerning the Lord's Supper, 1 Corinthians 11:27–29.

Read

- "Baptism: Fourth," *Small Catechism* (p. 340; SC IV, 11–14)
- "Baptism," *Large Catechism*, continued (pp. 429–31; LC IV, 64–86)

Discuss

11. What significance does Baptism continue to have in the daily lives of Christians (pp. 239–30; LC IV, 64–86)? See Romans 6:1–11; Galatians 3:26–29.

Sing

"To Jordan Came Our Lord," ELH 247, vv. 1–5
- *Lyrics*: M. Luther, tr. composite, ELH 247
- *Tune*: CHRIST UNSER HERR ZUM JORDAN KAM (ELH 247; CW 88; LBW 79; LSB 406; LW 223)
- *Alt. Tune*: ES WILL' UNS GOTT GENÄDIG SEIN (TLH 500)

1. To Jordan came our Lord, the Christ,
   The Father's will obeying.
   And there was by St. John baptized,
   All righteousness fulfilling.
   There He did consecrate a bath
   To wash away transgression,
   To rescue us from bitter death
   By His own blood and passion,
   New life for us creating!

2. So let us hear and ponder well
   What God creates in Baptism.
   What He would have us all believe,
   Who error shun and schism.
   That water at the font be used
   Is surely His good pleasure,
   Not water only, but the Word
   And Spirit without measure—
   He is the true Baptizer.

3. To show us this God speaks His Word,
   With sign and symbol given,
   On Jordan's banks was clearly heard
   The Father's voice from heaven:
   "This is my well-beloved Son,
   My soul's delight and treasure,
   Hear Him!" O hear Him ev'ry one!
   To save you is His pleasure.
   Hear and believe His teaching.

4. In Jordan's water God's own Son
   In sinless manhood bending,
   The Spirit, too, from heaven's throne,
   In dove-like form descending.
   This truth must never be denied,
   Our faith should never waver,
   That all Three Persons do preside
   At Baptism's holy laver,
   And dwell with each believer.

5. To His disciples Jesus said:
   "Go forth, teach every nation,
   For, lost in sin, all must repent,
   And flee from condemnation.
   All who believe and are baptized
   Shall thereby have salvation."
   Thus, born again in Jesus Christ
   We're freed from sin's damnation.
   We shall inherit heaven.

Remember

Baptism is a holy work that God Himself performs when His Word makes ordinary water into a spiritual washing. This washing, or "Baptism," distributes the forgiveness of sins that Christ won on the cross; brings to life those who are spiritually dead; and, marks for eternal salvation the children of God. Baptism accomplishes these things because Christ, who instituted Baptism, promises in His Word that Baptism accomplishes these things. Christ never assigned an age qualification for Baptism; its benefits apply to infants as well as to adults. Throughout their lives, believers should remember their Baptism and draw encouragement from the promises that God graciously applied to them at their Baptism —promises of forgiveness, rebirth, and eternal life.

Lesson 11:
Receiving the True Body and Blood of Our Lord

Pray

O Lord Jesus Christ, we thank You, that of Your infinite mercy You have instituted this Your Sacrament, in which we eat Your body and drink Your blood: Grant us, we beseech You, by Your Holy Spirit, that we may not receive this gift unworthily, but that we may confess our sins, remember Your agony and death, believe the forgiveness of sin, and day by day grow in faith and love, until we obtain eternal salvation; through You, who live and reign with the Father and the Holy Spirit, one true God, now and forever. Amen.

Veit Dietrich, Collect for Maundy Thursday, in *ELH*, Collect #57, p. 154.

Read

* "The Sacrament of the Altar: Essence," *Small Catechism* (p. 343; SC VI, 1–4)
* "The Sacrament of the Altar," *Large Catechism* (pp. 431–34; LC V, 1–19)

Discuss

1. To where should people direct their attention in order to have a correct understanding of the Lord's Supper (LC V, 4–7)? See 1 Corinthians 11:23–26.

2. Which words or phrases in the following Scripture passages indicate that some of the information conveyed in these passages should be understood figuratively rather than literally? See Genesis 40:8; Daniel 2:45; Matthew 13:3,10,13,31,34,35; Revelation 1:10,16,19–20.

3. Does the context surrounding the words of institution in Matthew 26:17–30 include any indicators that the language should be taken figuratively, such as in the case of a parable or a vision? Would a dying man who is bequeathing his last will and testament to his most beloved friends speak in uncertain figures of speech without making it crystal clear what he really meant, or would he instead speak plainly and simply in a direct and literal manner?

4. What, according to the plain sense of the words of institution, is the essence of the Sacrament of the Altar (LC V, 8–9)?

5. How do sacramentally consecrated bread and wine differ from ordinary bread and wine (LC V, 10–14)?

6. Is the Lord's Supper valid when administered by a hypocritical pastor (LC V, 15–19)? What comfort do you find in this truth?

Read

- "The Sacrament of the Altar: Benefits and Power," *Small Catechism* (p. 343; SC VI, 5–8)
- "The Sacrament of the Altar," *Large Catechism* (pp. 434–35; LC V, 20–32)

Discuss

7. What benefit does God provide for His people in the Lord's Supper (LC V, 20–27)?

8. How do the benefits distributed in the Lord's Supper relate to the benefits won by Christ on the cross (LC V, 28–32)? See, for an analogy to preaching, Romans 10:17; 1 Corinthians 1:21.

Read

- "The Sacrament of the Altar: Reception," *Small Catechism* (p. 343; SC VI, 9–10)
- "The Sacrament of the Altar," *Large Catechism* (pp. 435–40; LC V, 33–87)

Discuss

9. Who is worthy to receive the Lord's Supper, and who is unworthy (LC V, 33–38, 55–63)? See 1 Corinthians 11:27–29.

10. How often should a person receive the Lord's Supper (LC V, 39–54)? See Luke 22:19; 1 Corinthians 11:28; 2 Corinthians 13:5.

11. What, in addition to God's command and promise, should urge a person to come to the Lord's Supper (LC V, 71–84)? See Matthew 9:12; Romans 7:18–19; Ephesians 6:10–17.

12. What responsibilities do parents—fathers in particular—have with respect to the Lord's Supper (LC V, 85–87)? See Matthew 28:19–20; Ephesians 6:4.

Sing

"O Lord, We Praise Thee," ELH 327

- *Lyrics*: German folk hymn, 15th cent., v. 1; M. Luther, vv. 2–3, tr. composite, TLH 313
- *Tune*: *GOTT SEI GELOBET UND GEBENEDEIET* (ELH 327; CW 317; LBW 215; LHy 156; LSB 617; LW 238; TLH 313)

1. O Lord, we praise Thee, bless Thee, and adore Thee,
   In thanksgiving bow before Thee.
   Thou with Thy body and Thy blood dost nourish
   Our weak souls that they may flourish.
   O Lord, have mercy!
   May Thy body, Lord, born of Mary,
   That our sins and sorrows did carry,
   And Thy blood for us plead
   In all trial, fear, and need:
   O Lord, have mercy!

2. Thy holy body into death was given,
   Life to win for us in heaven.
   No greater love than this to Thee could bind us;
   May this feast thereof remind us!
   O Lord, have mercy!
   Lord, Thy kindness did so constrain Thee
   That Thy blood should bless and sustain me.
   All our debt Thou hast paid;
   Peace with God once more is made.
   O Lord, have mercy!

3. May God bestow on us His grace and favor
   To please Him with our behavior
   And live as brethren here in love and union
   Nor repent this blest Communion!
   O Lord, have mercy!
   Let not Thy good Spirit forsake us;
   Grant that heavn'ly minded He make us;
   Give Thy Church, Lord, to see
   Days of peace and unity:
   O Lord, have mercy!

Remember

Christ, and no one else, instituted the Lord's Supper. His words of institution determine what the sacrament is, whom it benefits, and how. He spoke those words as a final will and testament on the very night in which He knew He would soon be betrayed into death. He instructed His disciples to "do this in remembrance of Me," and so the church recognizes His divine lordship and follows His gracious invitation to the Holy Supper.

Mysteriously, Christ's body and blood, which were given and shed on the cross for the forgiveness of sins, are present in the bread and wine that are consecrated, distributed, and received according to His Word. Those who receive this Holy Supper worthily do so by recognizing their own unworthiness and by trusting in Christ's gracious invitation to receive His body and blood for their salvation. Those who fail to recognize His body and blood nonetheless receive it, but to their judgment rather than to their blessing. God's command and promise, and our own sinfulness and guilt, should draw us frequently back to the Lord's Table. There we participate anew in the victory that Christ our Passover Lamb won for us through His perfect life, His innocent death, and His glorious resurrection.

LESSON 12:
Assured of Forgiveness and
Empowered to Serve God

Pray

Lord God, heavenly Father, we beseech You so to guide and direct us by Your Holy Spirit that we may not forget our sins and be filled with pride, but continue in daily repentance and renewal, seeking comfort only in the blessed knowledge that You will be merciful to us, forgive us our sins, and grant us eternal life; through Your beloved Son, Jesus Christ, our Lord, who lives and reigns with you and the Holy Spirit, one true God, now and forever. Amen.

Veit Dietrich, Collect for the Eleventh Sunday after Trinity, in *ELH*, Collect #103, p. 161.

Read

- "How the Unlearned Should Be Taught to Confess" and "A Brief Form of Confession," *Small Catechism* (p. 341–42; SC V)
- "A Brief Exhortation to Confession," in *Concordia,* pp. 649–53

Discuss

1. Luther begins by insisting that confession should be voluntary. Identify the three abuses he discovered in the church of his day with respect to confession (Brief Exhortation, 1–4).

2. Luther next identifies a new problem that developed after the requirement of confession was removed from the churches. What was that danger (Brief Exhortation, 5–7)?

3. What are the three kinds of confession that Luther identifies, and how do you envision each of these as being helpful for your walk with God in Christ (Brief Exhortation, 8–14)?

4. Of what two parts does confession consist, and which of these two parts is more valuable (SC V; Brief Exhortation, 15–19)? See 1 John 1:8–2:2.

5. On what basis should a person be encouraged to confess his or her sins to a pastor or Christian friend (Brief Exhortation, 20–24)? See Matthew 16:16–19; John 20:19–23.

6. What warning does Luther provide for those who do not go to confession (Brief Exhortation, 25–29)? See 1 Corinthians 5:1–5,11.

7. How, finally, does Luther seek to strike the proper balance between coercion and laxity with respect to confession (Brief Exhortation, 30–35)? What, on the basis of Scripture, would you tell or ask Martin Luther about this topic if you could have a conversation with him today?

8. Which sins should a person confess, and how might the answer differ depending upon to whom the confession is being made (SC V)? See Psalm 19:12–14; Matthew 18:15–18.

Read

- "Daily Prayers" and "Table of Duties," *Small Catechism* (pp. 344–48)

Discuss

9. Review the Table of Duties that Luther collected from various New Testament epistles (SC Table of Duties). Identify weaknesses in your life, confessing the sins you commit against your vocation and asking God for strength to amend your life. Recognize also the manner in which Christ works in and through you, as a blessing to yourself and the people around you.

10. What elements in Luther's prayers for morning and evening make these good models for your own prayer life (SC Morning Prayer and Evening Prayer)?

11. How do Luther's suggestions for mealtime prayers fit with the First Commandment, the Second Commandment, the First Article, and the Fourth Petition (SC Daily Prayers)? How do they remind you also of the Gospel message encapsulated in the Second Article and packaged in the earthly elements of Holy Baptism and the Lord's Supper?

12. Formulate a plan for teaching the chief doctrines of Holy Scripture, which Luther's catechisms summarize, to the people whom God has entrusted to your care, such as your spouse, your children, your neighbors, or your Sunday school students.

Sing

"Out of the Depths I Cry to Thee," ELH 452
- *Lyrics*: M. Luther, tr. *The New Congregational Hymn Book*, 1859, vv. 1,5; C. Winkworth, vv. 2–4, alt., ELH 452
- *Tune*: AUS TIEFER NOT (ELH 452; CW 305; LBW 295; LHy 273; LSB 607; LW 230; TLH 329)

1. Out of the depths I cry to Thee;
   Lord, hear me I implore Thee!
   Thy graciouis ear incline to me;
   My prayer let come before Thee.

On my misdeeds in mercy look,
O deign to blot them from Thy book,
Or who can stand before Thee?

2. Thy love and grace alone avail
   To blot out my transgression;
   The best and holiest deeds must fail
   To break sin's dread oppression.
   Before Thee none can boasting stand,
   But all must fear Thy strict demand
   And live alone by mercy.

3. Therefore my hope is in the Lord
   And not in mine own merit;
   It rests upon His faithful Word
   To them of contrite spirit
   That He is merciful and just—
   This is my comfort and my trust.
   His help I wait with patience.

4. And though it tarry till the night
   And till the morning waken,
   My heart shall never doubt His might
   Nor count itself forsaken.
   Do thus, O ye of Israel's seed,
   Ye of the Spirit born indeed;
   Wait for your God's appearing.

5. Where'er the greatest sins abound,
   By grace they are exceeded;
   Thy helping hand is always found
   With aid where aid is needed.
   Our Shepherd good and true is He
   Who will at last His Israel free
   From all their sin and sorrow.

Remember

God the Father graciously forgives our sins for the sake of Jesus Christ, whose life, death, and resurrection accomplished our salvation. God the Holy Spirit distributes the benefits of this salvation to us through the Means of Grace. Absolution is one of these means. Like the preached Word, it proclaims that our sins are forgiven. Like the sacramental Word, it communicates the Gospel message in a tangible way. Absolution means that an earthly representative of God—usually a pastor—forgives us by the command and in the stead of God. Absolution provides specific comfort to individuals who feel burdened by, and therefore verbally confess, particular sins that have vexed them. Absolution speaks pure grace; it does not attach conditions or demand works of merit, but simply comforts the sin-sick soul with the Gospel: that Christ alone has fully atoned for all sins, period.

Purified by Word and Sacrament, and refreshed by Holy Absolution, Christians walk forth in newness of life. Through their vocations, Christians serve their neighbors in thanksgiving to God their Savior. Through daily prayer, they seek God's blessings constantly, both for themselves and for others in their midst. Having been forgiven much, they eagerly go forth to forgive others.

Scripture Index

About the Hausvater Project

The Hausvater Project is a nonprofit organization, founded in 2008, that promotes a biblical vision for family, church, and society in the spirit of the Lutheran confessions.

The organization seeks to equip Christian men and women for distinctive and complementary vocations in family, church, and society, by fostering research and education in light of Holy Scripture as proclaimed by the Lutheran Confessions.

For more information, visit:

www.hausvater.org

Contact:

info@hausvater.org

www.hausvater.org/contact

Follow us:

www.facebook.com/hausvaterproject

www.twitter.com/hausvater

About the Author / Speaking Engagements

Dr. Ryan C. MacPherson (Ph.D., University of Notre Dame) is a homeschool parent who has taught both children's Sunday school and adult Bible classes. He presently serves as chair of the History Department at Bethany Lutheran College and also is the founding president of the Hausvater Project, a nonprofit organization promoting a biblical vision for family, church, and society in the spirit of the Lutheran confessions. His publications include *Telling the Next Generation: The Evangelical Lutheran Synod's Vision for Christian Education, 1918–2011 and Beyond* (managing editor, 2011) and *The Culture of Life: Ten Essential Principles for Christian Bioethics* (2012).

Dr. MacPherson is a nationally featured speaker for religious organizations, academic associations, and public policy forums. He is a member of the Lutherans for Life speakers bureau and also has been interviewed on Pastor Todd Wilken's "Issues, Etc." radio program. Dr. MacPherson's expertise includes Christian education, religion and politics, religion and science, bioethics, and the family in public policy.

For more information, visit:

www.ryancmacpherson.com

To schedule Dr. MacPherson for a speaking engagement:

www.ryancmacpherson.com/contact

Follow Dr. MacPherson online:

www.facebook.com/ryancmacphersonphd

www.linkedin.com/in/ryancmacpherson

www.twitter.com/ryancmacpherson

The Culture of Life

**"I have come that they may have life,
and that they may have it more abundantly." (John 10:10)**

Ryan C. MacPherson, Ph.D.

Designed for both individual and group study, this book outlines the culture of life in sharp contrast to the culture of death. Grounded in Holy Scripture, oriented by the forgiving love of Jesus Christ, and motivated by compassion for people in all of life's stages, *The Culture of Life* guides readers through today's most controversial topics in bioethics, including:

- abortion and infanticide
- euthanasia ("mercy killing") and physician-assisted suicide
- chastity, marriage, parenting, and elder care

"Positive, biblical, confessional, Christ-centered—all the things I love to see from Lutherans on these issues."

James I. Lamb, M.Div., D.Min.
Executive Director, Lutherans For Life

"Dr. MacPherson has done a wonderful job of gleaning ten vital bioethical principles from the Scriptures and the Lutheran Confessions. This book should be an important resource for pastors, teachers, and Bible class leaders who need a content-rich resource to help them instruct others about life issues from a traditional, Christian perspective."

Rev. Dr. Kevin E. Voss
Director, Concordia Bioethics Institute of Concordia University Wisconsin

The Culture of Life

"There are two ways," taught the early Christians, "one of life and one of death; but a great difference between the two ways." So began the *Didache*, a discipleship tract circulated within a century or so after Christ's resurrection. . . .

The culture of life traces its origin to the Holy and Most Blessed Trinity—Father, Son, and Holy Spirit—who said:

> "Let Us make man in Our image." . . . So God created man in His own image; in the image of God He created him; male and female He created them. (Genesis 1:26–27) . . .

Just as the culture of life cherishes God's work of creation, so also the culture of life celebrates the special work to which God calls a husband and wife: procreation, the begetting of offspring. . . .

The culture of life flows from marriage as God instituted it: a lifelong union of a man and a woman that celebrates sexual complementarity, children, and chastity. The culture of life proclaims that marriage establishes and defines society, not the other way around. And marriage truly *is*—not merely is *thought* by some people to be, but rather marriage *is*—the divinely established lifelong union of a man and a woman, a union that celebrates sexual complementarity, children, and chastity. . . .

In, with, and under fatherhood and motherhood,

God the Heavenly Father distributes His blessings of daily bread, both physical and spiritual. Amazingly, God blesses people even through inadequate earthly parents. God calls upon us, therefore, to respect the office of parenthood and to recognize, even in the quirky personalities of some parents, the divine office of parental blessings—what Luther called "a majesty there hidden" (Large Catechism I, 106). Recognizing God's special callings for both fathers and mothers, *the culture of life honors parents. . . .*

The culture of life respects human life at all its stages, recognizing that those who have lived long and well have much to offer those who are just beginning their journeys on this earth. Not only should the young respect the aging, but the elderly should also respect themselves with the honor God says is due them. If Grandpa is too weak to work, he is not too weak to pray. Let us cherish our parents and grandparents as they intercede on our behalf and pass down to their children's children the wisdom of the Lord. . . .

The culture of life does not lose hope, not even on the gloomiest of days. The culture of life stands atop the dark mountain of Calvary on Holy Friday confident that in the midst of suffering there will be healing, that in the midst of death there will be life. The culture of life prays in vigil for the first signs of dawn on Easter morning, eager to discover—and ready to proclaim to others—that Christ has triumphed over the grave. . . .

The culture of life is the culture of repentance and forgiveness. . . . The culture of life looks to Christ alone.

www.hausvater.org/books

Ordering Information

Studying Luther's Large Catechism is available for individual purchase at Amazon.com and other reputable booksellers. The author receives no royalties; all net proceeds support the nonprofit mission of the Hausvater Project.

Significant price discounts are available for bulk orders by churches and schools.

For further information:

info@hausvater.org

www.hausvater.org/books

CPSIA information can be obtained
at www.ICGtesting.com
Printed in the USA
BVHW070406210121
598273BV00004B/423